Founded
on the Rock

[the vital basis for success, safety
and a life that pleases God]

by   Derek   Prince

BOOKS BY DEREK PRINCE

DPM-UK • Kingsfield • Hadrian Way •
Baldock • SG7 6AN • Herts • UK

Founded

on the Rock

[the vital basis for success, safety
and a life that pleases God]

by   Derek   Prince

DEREK PRINCE MINISTRIES - UK
KINGSFIELD, HADRIAN WAY, BALDOCK,
SG7 6AN, HERTS, UK

FOUNDED ON THE ROCK

© 2007 Derek Prince Ministries–International
This edition DPM-UK 2011

Published by DPM-UK
Kingsfield, Hadrian Way,
Baldock SG7 6AN, UK
www.dpmuk.org

ISBN 978-1-901144-65-9
Product code: B100
Printed in the United Kingdom

Scripture quotations are from the New King James Version of the Bible,
Thomas Nelson Publishers, Nashville, TN, © 1982.

This book was compiled from the extensive archive of Derek Prince's un-
published materials and edited by the Derek Prince Ministries editorial team.

DEREK PRINCE MINISTRIES
WWW.DPMUK.ORG

Founded on the Rock

The Bible is a model of good teaching and it follows various principles of teaching. One in particular is that it starts from the known to lead people on to the unknown. It never starts with the un-known, it starts with what is known and proceeds from there to the unknown. One of the ways the Bible does this is to take very simple, familiar, everyday experiences and activities and give them a spiritual application.

There are various examples. The Bible speaks about a farmer sowing his seed, about a fisherman catching fish in a dragnet or a soldier putting on his armor. In a completely different kind of context, it speaks about a bride preparing herself for her wedding. Those are just a few examples of this principle.

The Christian Life—A Building

The particular, familiar activity I want to focus on is that of constructing a building. This picture of the Christian life is used at least as many times as any other picture in the Bible.

We are going to turn, first of all, to the epistle of Jude, which is a word of exhortation to us as believers.

> *But you, beloved, building yourselves up on your most holy faith, praying in the Holy Spirit, keep yourselves in the love of God.*
>
> *Jude 20–21*

Scripture says here that we must build ourselves up in our most holy faith. It is one of the ways in which this metaphor of building applies. We are responsible to build ourselves up.

Then in Ephesians 2 it speaks about a holy temple in the Lord:

> . . . in whom the whole building, being fitted together, grows into a holy temple in the Lord, in whom you also are being built together for a dwelling place of God in the Spirit.
>
> Ephesians 2:21–22

Speaking about the collective Christian community, we are to be built together in the Holy Spirit as a place for God to dwell.

Then, speaking about Jesus as a living stone, Peter says:

> Coming to Him [Jesus] as to a living stone, rejected indeed by men, but chosen by God and precious, you also, as living stones, are being built up a spiritual house, a holy priesthood, to offer up spiritual sacrifices acceptable to God through Jesus Christ.
>
> 1 Peter 2:4–5

There we are compared, each one of us, to living stones that are being built together into a holy temple that the Lord is going to occupy.

Let's look at one final example from Acts 20. It is the farewell of Paul to the Ephesian elders whom he loved with a special love because it was in Ephesus that his ministry had perhaps the greatest impact of any other place.

In his speech in Acts 20, Paul is saying farewell and telling them they will never see him again in this life. It was a very moving situation for all of them. This is really the final exhortation he wanted to leave with them:

So now, brethren, I commend you to God and
to the word of His grace, which is able to build
you up and give you an inheritance among all
those who are sanctified.

Acts 20:32

Paul is telling us that the main means for building us up is the word of God's grace, the Bible. He says it is able to build us up and to give us an inheritance among all those who are set apart for Jesus Christ by faith in Him.

The Foundation Is Jesus

I am not a builder, but I know one thing: In any permanent building, whether it is built of brick or stone, concrete or timber, the vital area is the foundation. The Bible deals specifically with this, and it is an issue of great importance for every one of us.

The foundation sets limits to the building that may be built above it—both in size and in weight. The foundation sets the limits, and this also is true in the Christian life. You cannot build a more successful Christian life than your foundation will permit. This is the vital issue: What is your foundation? Have you laid the right foundation?

There is only one foundation that is adequate and all-sufficient. It is the person of Jesus Christ. Paul, writing to the Corinthian Christians, uses two metaphors. He uses the agricultural metaphor but then goes on to use the building metaphor.

For we are God's fellow workers [working together with God]; *you are God's field* [that is the agricultural metaphor and] *you are God's building* [that is the construction metaphor]. *According to the grace of God which was given to me, as a wise master builder* [Greek, "architect"] *I have laid the foundation, and another builds on it. But let each one take heed how he builds on it. For no other*

foundation can anyone lay than that which is laid,
which is Jesus Christ.

1 Corinthians 3:9–11

Paul says there is only one foundation for the Christian life and that is Jesus Himself. Anything that is not built on that foundation will not stand the test of time and of trial. So, it is very important for every one of us to assess what our life is built on. Are we truly built on the Lord Jesus Christ? Do we have a personal relationship and a knowledge of Jesus that makes us able to relate personally to Him?

The question of laying this foundation in Jesus is extremely important, so I want to take some time to deal with the issue of how we can have this foundation—the foundation of Jesus—in our lives. I would invite each reader to examine his or her own life—your spiritual condition and spiritual experience—and check as to whether your relationship with the foundation is right.

Let's begin in Matthew 16 with some basic teaching. Jesus is talking to His disciples:

When Jesus came into the region of Caesarea Philippi, He asked His disciples, saying, "Who do men say that I, the Son of Man, am?" So they said, "Some say John the Baptist, some Elijah, and others Jeremiah or one of the prophets." [Then He makes it very personal.] *He said to them, "But who do you say that I am?" Simon Peter answered and said, "You are the Christ* [Messiah], *the Son of the living God." Jesus answered and said to him, "Blessed are you, Simon Bar-Jonah, for flesh and blood has not revealed this to you, but My Father who is in heaven. And I also say to you that you are Peter, and on this rock I will build My church, and the gates of Hades shall not prevail against it."*

Matthew 16:13–18

This was a crucial moment in the life of Peter and in the whole history of Christianity. Jesus used this encounter with Peter to establish the way in which we can lay a foundation in Jesus Christ Himself.

It has often been suggested that Peter is the foundation of the church. I would have to say, if it were so it would be a very wobbly building—because a little later Jesus rebukes Peter by saying, *"Get behind Me, Satan"* (Matthew 16:23). Later still, Peter denied the Lord three times (John 18:15–17, 25–27). Even after the resurrection Paul had to rebuke him for compromising with the truth of the gospel for fear of his fellow Jews. (See Galatians 2:11–16.) I, for one, am grateful that the church is not built on Peter—nor on me!

What actually emerges from this passage, which is very clear in the Greek testament (which is the original version that we have), "You are Peter [*petros*], and on this rock [*petra*] I will build My church" (Matthew 16:18). *Petros* in Greek means a stone or at most a boulder, nothing bigger than that. Normally it would be the kind of stone that people would take up to stone someone with.

On the other hand, *petra* means a jagged rock that extends from the bedrock. It is often used to describe a cliff or something on that scale. The important thing to remember is it is part of the bedrock. What is the bedrock? It is just what Peter had been going through: the recognition of Jesus for who He is, revealed only by the Holy Spirit. No one can know Jesus and who He really is unless God the Father by the Holy Spirit reveals Him.

This is the *petra*—it is the bedrock on which our Christian faith must be based. It is a personal encounter and a personal revelation of Jesus—not as the carpenter's Son, not as a historical figure, but as the eternal, uncreated Son of God. That is where we have to come if we are going to build on that rock. The experience through which Peter passed must be paralleled in our experience.

I have told people many times, "You can join a church, you can go through a religious ceremony, or you can say a prayer and still not be changed. But if you really encounter

Jesus, you will be changed. No one encounters Jesus and remains the same." Each of us needs to ask: Have I ever had this life-changing, personal encounter with the Lord Jesus Christ?

Encountering Jesus

I would like to suggest four successive phases through which Peter passed in his encounter of Jesus.

First of all, confrontation. Jesus and Peter met face to face. There was no mediator, no priest, no one between them. It was a direct, personal confrontation of Jesus. That is what our experience should be, too. Jesus said in another place, "I am the door. If anyone enters by Me, he will be saved" (John 10:9). There is only one way into the kingdom of God—through the door. The door is not a church; it is not a doctrine; it is Jesus. "I am the door."

Second, the confrontation was followed by revelation, a revelation granted by God the Father through the Holy Spirit. Jesus said, "Flesh and blood has not revealed this" (Matthew 16:17). You cannot arrive at it by your natural senses, there has to be a revelation. This is essential. No one can know Jesus as He truly is in His eternal Sonship of God without a personal revelation. You can study theology, you can go to a Bible college, you can even become a minister. But without this personal revelation of Jesus, you cannot know Him. The revelation comes only from God the Father through Jesus Christ the Son.

Have you had that personal encounter with Jesus? I have. More than fifty years ago in the middle of the night in an Army barrack room during World War II, I encountered Jesus. I had no doctrinal knowledge, no evangelical language. I could not even say I was "saved" or "born again." I learned all that later. But I was changed—radically and permanently changed. I was not made perfect—in fact, let me confess to you, I am still not perfect. But I was changed for the better.

The third step is, there has to be an acknowledgment of what the Holy Spirit shows us. We have to say, "Yes, I believe. I receive." We have to make some kind of response. It is not automatic; it requires something happening in us.

And fourth, there has to be a public confession of our faith in Jesus. That is what Jesus drew out of Peter: "You are the Christ [Messiah]" (Matthew 16:16). Peter made it public. People speak about "secret believers," and I acknowledge there are secret believers, especially in countries where acknowledgement of that fact would mean being put to death. But nobody can permanently remain a secret believer, for Jesus said:

> *"Therefore, whoever confesses Me before men, him I will also confess before My Father who is in heaven. But whoever denies Me before men, him I will also deny before My Father who is in heaven."*
> *Matthew 10:32–33*

Jesus in His characteristic way does not give us three choices, only two. We either confess or we deny. If we fail to confess in an appropriate situation, we are, in effect, denying. So, each one of us at some point has to come to the place where we openly acknowledge our faith in the Lord Jesus Christ. This is a critical moment for many.

I discovered in the army after I had become a believer that the best thing to do was to let everybody know the first moment you met them where you stand. Then you never have to go back and say, "I didn't really tell you at the beginning, but . . ." So, I did something every night in the barrack room, which is not just a religious act. Wherever I was, I would kneel down at my bed and pray. That revealed just what kind of person they were dealing with. It was much easier that way. I saw other Christians who waffled, who did not come right out and say what they believed, and it was much harder for them to go back afterwards and make the right confession.

I want to recommend that practice. We do not have to stand on a street corner and preach, we do not have to be a teacher. We can be housewives or students, but wherever we are, we should let people know we believe in Jesus, that He is the Son of God.

Let me just review those four successive phases of this encounter, which is so basic. This is how we lay the foundation of Jesus in our lives personally.

First, there was a confrontation.

Second, there was a revelation granted by God the Father through the Holy Spirit.

Third, Peter responded with an acknowledgment.

And fourth, he made a public confession.

What About Today?

The question might arise: Is such a revelation possible today? Is it possible for people like you and me to know Jesus just as genuinely and just as personally as Peter and the other disciples did?

We need to see two important things. First of all, Jesus was not revealed to Peter as the Son of the carpenter. He had known Him that way for quite awhile. Jesus was revealed to Peter as the eternal Son of God. The Scripture says in Hebrews 13:8:

Jesus Christ is the same yesterday, today and forever.

There has been no change in Him; there never will be. So, it is not a question of language, culture or clothing, but it is a question of the eternal person of Jesus. That is what Peter encountered; maybe for the first time in his life. Peter really had a revelation of who Jesus is.

Second, the revelation was granted through the Holy Spirit. The Bible calls the Holy Spirit the eternal Spirit, the timeless Spirit. Time, fashion, history, customs, language—they do not change the Holy Spirit.

For those two reasons it is equally possible for you and me to have this direct, personal revelation of Jesus, just as it was possible for Peter. First of all, because it is the eternal

Son of God who is revealed; and secondly, because it is the eternal Spirit who reveals Him.

Building on the Foundation

We come now to the next important practical issue: if we have laid the foundation, how do we proceed to build on it? You remember that the metaphors we cited at the beginning of this study all spoke about building. So the next vitally important and practical issue is how to build on the foundation.

For this, I want to look at a well-known parable of Jesus—a parable about the wise man and the foolish man. Each of them built a house, but they built it different ways.

> *"Therefore whoever hears these sayings of Mine, and does them, I will liken him to a wise man who built his house on the rock* [the bedrock, petra]: *and the rain descended, the floods came, and the winds blew and beat on that house; and it did not fall, for it was founded on the rock. But everyone who hears these sayings of Mine, and does not do them, will be like a foolish man who built his house on the sand: and the rain descended, the floods came, and the winds blew and beat on that house; and it fell. And great was its fall."*
>
> *Matthew 7:24–27*

First of all, it is important to see that each house was subjected to the same test. Neither house was free from being tested. The same storm that hit one house hit the other. The Christian life is not a storm-free life. We will go through storms. God has never guaranteed that we will not. In fact, Paul and Barnabas said to the early church, "We must through many tribulations enter the kingdom of God" (Acts 14:22). If we are on a road that has no tribulation, it is questionable whether it leads to the kingdom of God, because that is what Paul said.

It is not in the scope of this message to explain why we go through tribulation but, believe me, God has a purpose in it. If someone is going through it now, don't give up. God will bring you through and you will find at the end that He has dealt with you and taught you things you could not learn any other way. I know that from personal experience.

The wise man builds in two ways: by hearing and doing the words of Jesus, the words of the Bible. How can we build on the foundation? In just the same way: by hearing what the Bible says and doing it. We cannot be just a hearer only, because the Bible has no promises for them, but only for the hearer and doer. It is practical. It is applying the teaching of the Bible and the teaching of Jesus in our own lives. We find as we go on in this that God will continually open up new areas in which we need to apply the truth.

I have been a Christian now for more than fifty years, but God is continually showing me new ways in which to apply His Word—new areas of my life in which I need to apply it. My building is not complete; it is still being built. But I thank God it has passed through a number of storms successfully.

Dig Deep

Another parable of Jesus is very similar, but there is an important addition. Jesus says:

> *"But why do you call Me 'Lord, Lord,' and do not do the things which I say?"*
>
> *Luke 6:46*

That is an important question. It is futile to call Jesus "Lord" if you do not obey Him, because the very title means someone who is to be obeyed. Jesus wants us to beware of just having a vocal confession that does not affect the way we live. He goes on:

"Whoever comes to Me, and hears My sayings and

does them, I will show you whom he is like: He is like a man building a house, who dug deep and laid the foundation on the rock. And when the flood arose, the stream beat vehemently against that house, and could not shake it, for it was founded on the rock [the bedrock, the petra]. *But he who heard and did nothing is like a man who built a house on the earth without a foundation, against which the stream beat vehemently; and immediately it fell. And the ruin of that house was great."*

verses 47–49

There is one important detail added in Luke which is not in Matthew. I wonder how many noticed it? It says the man who wanted to reach the bedrock had to dig deep. He had to get a lot of things out of the way before he could build on the bedrock.

That is also true with many of us. For most of us who grew up in a nominal Christian culture, there are a lot of hindrances and influences we must get out of the way before we reach the bedrock. Others who have grown up in a completely non-Christian culture will have to eliminate things, too, but they will be different. I want to suggest five hindrances that we need to dig out of the way.

Tradition

Now, not all traditions are bad. Some are good. We do not want to throw out all tradition. However, Jesus said to the people of His day, "You have made the commandment of God of no effect by your tradition" (Matthew 15:6). Even if we believe in traditions and act on them, it does not mean they are in line with the Scripture. According to my observation, Jesus would say exactly the same thing to the same Jewish people today. "By your traditions you have made the Word of God of no effect." But let's not just look at the Jews. This is also true of many others of Christian backgrounds. We have inherited traditions, ways of acting, things we do, words we speak, which are not necessarily in line with Scripture. So we must be very careful to check these out.

Prejudice

The second hindrance we need to eliminate is prejudice. There is really no one who has not had some prejudice at one time or another. There are all sorts of prejudices, such as racial prejudices. Unfortunately, the world is full today of racial prejudices. We know in countries like South Africa, for instance, where racial prejudices eliminated certain people from being part of the church (where there has been a wonderful change, let me add). A terrible thought! But that is not the only area where there is racial prejudice. The United States of America has been full of racial prejudice and in many places still is today.

I am from a British background so I know the British people have their prejudices, too. I grew up with many of them. I have had to dig deep to get rid of them. My own family background is from India. All my forbears served with British forces in India. I remember as a boy of about twelve saying innocently at a lunch, "I don't see why you couldn't invite an Indian to lunch." The reaction was one of horror in my family. I thought, *What is the reason for this?* Well, later on I realized that is prejudice. Believe me, no matter what your racial background is, very few people are free from all racial prejudice.

There is denominational prejudice. Most of us react in a somewhat negative way to certain denominations. My first wife Lydia, who is with the Lord, was Danish. She grew up in the Danish Lutheran Church and then she did something that was terrible in their eyes. She was baptized as a believer—which they call in Danish "a second-time baptizer." In her case, because she was a teacher in the Danish state school system, she actually went before the Parliament so they could ascertain whether or not she could remain a teacher. Lydia continued to have a denominational prejudice with the Lutheran Church really to the end of her days. I do not justify that; I believe it was a weakness in her.

When I hear about people belonging to a certain denomination, I develop an attitude against them without ever having met them. I think, *Well, they're going to be like that, and this is where they're wrong"* and so on. Experience has taught me, if possible, that I should never judge a person till I have met them. I have met people from "wrong" denominational backgrounds who are some of the most "right" people I know. Also some who were from the "right" background who were wrong. So we must not give in to denominational prejudice.

Then there is social prejudice. Again, I am an example of somebody brought up with social prejudice, but I was not even aware of it. I just didn't know how the rest of the world lived. I was educated in Britain at Eton and then at Cambridge University. Then I got plunged into the British Army and I was together with all sorts of people I never had been together with. I began to realize how limited my knowledge of my own British people was. I thank God for that experience, five and a half years in the British Army; it cleansed me of a lot of social prejudices. Having been from a family of officers, I was used to being on that level, and when I was not on that level I learned something. When you see people from the same level, they look one way. But when you see them from below they look different. I have always tried to be sensitive to this, with the Lord's help.

There is also personal prejudice. Some people do not like others who have loud voices. Some people do not like people with red hair. There are all sorts of silly, personal prejudices most of us have. I have a prejudice against people who munch apples. I really fight it, but the prejudice is still there in the background because I just don't like that noise.

Preconception

The third hindrance to get out of the way are preconceptions. For instance, some people have a completely false view of who Jesus is: gentle Jesus, meek and mild, turning up at the Christmas party. That is not the real

Jesus. He was a very different kind of person, very shocking, and prone to eliminate our prejudices and preconceptions.

There are many other ways we can have preconceptions. For instance, preconceptions of what it would be like to be a Christian. Growing up, I thought to myself, *If I were to become a Christian, it would mean misery for the rest of my life.* Like Pat Boone, I thought, *Heaven isn't worth seventy years of misery on earth!* so I completely eliminated the possibility of being a Christian—until I met Jesus.

Unbelief

A fourth hindrance—and something that is very dangerous—is unbelief. Sometimes when I am going to teach I will begin by getting everyone to renounce unbelief, because many of us are still beset by unbelief in various areas. Our minds are not really open to faith.

Rebellion

Lastly, and I think the most important, is rebellion. We might say, "I'm not a rebel." Oh, yes, we are! And if we have not yet discovered it, we will go on being one. Every descendant of Adam is born with a rebel inside. We have to identify that rebel and deal with it. God has only got one remedy for the rebel—and that is execution! God does not send the rebel to church; He does not teach him the Golden Rule; and He does not have him memorize Scripture. God puts him to death! But the mercy of God is, the execution took place nearly two thousand years ago when Jesus died on the cross. *"Our old man was crucified with Him"* (Romans 6:6). We have to come to the place where we identify that rebel inside us and willingly submit to execution.

The Word of God

Now I come to the Bible because this is as important as anything else in the Christian life. What is our attitude to the Bible? Is it the same as that of Jesus? I just want to take one passage of John's gospel. Jesus said:

"If He [God] called them gods, to whom the word of
God came (and the Scripture cannot be broken)..."
John 10:35

This is a very significant verse because in it Jesus uses the two main titles for the Bible: the "word of God" and "the Scripture." When He calls the Bible "the Word of God," it means that it proceeded from God, not from man. It may have come through human channels, but it is a word that comes from God.

The phrase "the Scripture" is a limiting phrase. It means that which has been set down in writing. God has said many things which are not set down in writing. But by divine overruling the Bible contains those things God said that He saw needed to be set down in writing. That is the Scripture—that which is written.

Concerning that, Jesus made one, simple, sweeping statement: "The Scripture cannot be broken." We can argue as much as we like about the inspiration of the Bible or the authority of the Bible, but Jesus has said it all: It cannot be broken. It is absolutely authoritative. It will be totally fulfilled. Everything in it will be exactly worked out. We can take a stand against it and deny it, but we cannot break it. In fact, if we deny it, ultimately it will break us. The Scripture cannot be broken.

There is a type of study called "higher criticism," which subjects the Scriptures to all sorts of ridiculous fantasies and ends up by making it a totally ineffective book. If there is one thing the devil wants to do in our lives, it is to undermine our faith in the authority and accuracy of the Bible. But, if we are like Jesus, we simply say, *"The Scripture cannot be broken."*

Jesus Is the Word

Not only is the Bible the Word of God, but Jesus Himself is the Word of God. This comes out in John's gospel in two places:

*In the beginning was the Word, and the Word was
with God, and the Word was God.*

John 1:1

*And the Word became flesh and dwelt among us,
and we beheld His glory, the glory as of the only
begotten of the Father, full of grace and truth.*

John 1:14

That refers to Jesus. He was the Word, He is the
Word. When Jesus was born, the Word became flesh.
But He always was the Word. Eternally He was the Word
with God.

When He comes back, how is He coming back? What
will His name be? This is a picture of Jesus coming out of
heaven in glory to establish His kingdom on earth.

*Now I saw heaven opened, and behold, a white
horse. And He who sat on him was called Faithful
and True, and in righteousness He judges and
makes war. His eyes were like a flame of fire, and
on His head were many crowns* [diadems, royal
crowns]. *He had a name written that no one knew
except Himself. He was clothed with a robe dipped
in blood, and His name is called The Word of God.*

Revelation 19:11–13

This is truly remarkable in the sense that when He first
came He was the Word, and when He comes back He will
be the Word. He always was the Word, still is the Word and
will be the Word.

That brings out something very important. There is
total agreement between Jesus and the Bible. Our attitude
toward one is the attitude toward the other. We cannot
believe in Jesus and disbelieve the Bible. Can we absorb
that fact? Jesus is the Word of God—He is the Word made
flesh. The Bible is the Word in Scripture, or in writing. Our
attitude toward the one must be the same as our attitude

toward the other. There is total agreement between the two.

Five Vital Facts

I would now like to examine five vital facts about the Word of God and our relationship to it, which are contained in John's gospel, in just three verses. Jesus is, in a sense, taking farewell of His disciples. He is warning them that He is about to leave and they will be left on their own for a while. It is a very traumatic time for the disciples; they are overwhelmed with this revelation. But in the middle of it, Jesus gives a marvelous revelation of what the Bible should mean to us as believers. He says:

"A little while longer and the world will see Me no more, but you will see Me. Because I live, you will live also."

John 14:19

Jesus made a distinction there between the world—those who do not acknowledge Jesus—and His own disciples. He said the world would not see Him but the disciples would. Then Judas asked Him a very relevant question:

Judas (not Iscariot) said to Him, "Lord, how is it that You will manifest Yourself to us, and not to the world?" *verse22*

The answer Jesus gave is just full of important truth.

Jesus answered and said to him, "If anyone loves Me, he will keep My word; and My Father will love him, and We will come to him and make Our home with him." *verse23*

I want to bring out five vitally important facts in the answer of Jesus. First of all, Jesus said He would reveal Himself to His disciples, not to the world. What is the distinguishing mark between the disciples and the world? The answer is keeping the Word of God. True disciples keep the Word of Jesus. They are not marked out by denominational labels; they are marked out by the way they relate to the Word. That is what makes us, or otherwise prevents us, from being true disciples. It is our relationship to the Word of God. Keeping God's Word distinguishes disciples from the world.

In every congregation every one of us is in one or other of those two categories. If we are disciples, we keep the Word of God. If we do not keep the Word, we belong to the world—the world that is not under the Lordship of Jesus.

The second truth is, Jesus said, "If anyone loves Me, he will keep My Word." So, keeping God's Word is the supreme test of the disciple's love for God. Love is the motivation for obedience.

It is very important to understand that, as believers, we are not motivated by fear; we are motivated by love. In a certain sense, the Law used the motivation of fear: "If you do this, you will be punished." But that does not work. I have helped to raise a large number of children. I discovered that while children are under your control as a parent, you can use fear—but once they leave you, if they were motivated by fear, they will change. The only motivation that will keep them loyal and faithful is love. God and Jesus were wise enough not to build on fear but to build on love. Keeping God's Word is the supreme test of the disciple's love for God. Love is the motivation for obedience.

Then Jesus says, "If anyone loves Me, he will keep My Word, and My Father will love him." That is another wonderful fact. Keeping God's Word is what causes God the Father to love us with a special love. God loves the whole world in a certain way. But God has a very different degree and kind of love for true disciples of Jesus, for those who keep His Word.

Looking back to the question that Judas asked, "How is it that You will manifest Yourself to us, and not to the world?" we see Jesus' answer was, "If anybody loves Me, he will keep My Word." So, how does Christ manifest Himself to us? Through the Word. It is through the keeping of the Word that we get to know Jesus better. We could perhaps have some wonderful, spiritual experience—being caught up to the third heaven or something. But that does not happen to most people and it is not the basic way by which God reveals Himself and Jesus reveals Himself. It is through keeping the Word of God.

Finally, and this is an amazing statement: "If anyone loves Me . . . My Father will love him, and We will come to him and make Our home with him." There are only a very few places in the Bible where the plural pronoun is used about God, but this is one of them. Jesus says We—My Father and I—will come to him and make our home with him. That is a breathtaking statement, an amazing revelation that God the Father and God the Son want to come and make their dwelling with us. They want to make us their personal abode. But how does it come about? Through the Word. If we are not lovers of the Word, if we are not obedient to the Word, God will not make His dwelling place with us.

Let me say this as I close, and it is a very solemn thought: We do not love God more than we love His Word. So if we want to know how much we really love God, how much place God has in our life, we can find out. It is not something we need to speculate about. Just ask yourself these questions: How much do I love the Bible? How much place does the Bible have in my life? Because that is as much as you love God and that is as much place as you give to God in your life.

Let me summarize those five statements about the Bible because they are crucial. So many Christians are in a kind of twilight zone, they do not really know what is light and what is darkness. They wish and they hope, but they are not really sure. It is because they have not given the Word of God its rightful place in their lives.

1.   Keeping God's Word distinguishes true disciples from the world.

2. Keeping God's Word is the supreme test of the disciple's love for God. Love is our motivation for obedience, not fear.

3. Keeping God's Word is the supreme cause of God's love for the disciple. God loves disciples in a special way. He loves the whole world, but He has a special love for disciples. But, those whom He loves as disciples are those who keep God's Word. If we want to be specially dear to God, then we have to keep His Word.

4. Through God's Word, kept and obeyed, Christ manifests Himself to us. The question was, "How will You manifest Yourself to us, and not to the world?" Jesus said, "If you love Me, you will keep My Word. That is how I will manifest Myself."

5. Finally, through God's Word, the Father and the Son will come together to indwell us. That is an amazing thought that just takes my breath away. God the Father and God the Son want to make their dwelling with us. But they will only do it as we keep God's Word.

Heavenly Father, thank You for Your Word—the Word of God, the Bible. This sure, authoritative, infallible Word is a lamp for our feet and a light for our path. I pray, Lord, for everyone who ultimately is confronted by this message, that You will cause us to be lovers of Your Word. That You, by Your grace, will enable us to give Your Word, the Bible, its rightful place in our lives that we may be truly disciples of the Lord Jesus.

• • • • •

ABOUT THE AUTHOR

Derek Prince (1915–2003) was born in India of British parents. Educated as a scholar of Greek and Latin at Eton College and Cambridge University, England, he held a Fellowship in Ancient and Modern Philosophy at King's College. He also studied several modern languages, including Hebrew and Aramaic, at Cambridge University and the Hebrew University in Jerusalem.

While serving with the British army in World War II, he began to study the Bible and experienced a life-changing encounter with Jesus Christ. Out of this encounter he formed two conclusions: first, that Jesus Christ is alive; second, that the Bible is a true, relevant, up-to-date book. These conclusions altered the whole course of his life, which he then devoted to studying and teaching the Bible.

Derek's main gift of explaining the Bible and its teaching in a clear and simple way has helped build a foundation of faith in millions of lives. His non-denominational, non-sectarian approach has made his teaching equally relevant and helpful to people from all racial and religious backgrounds.

He is the author of over 50 books, 600 audio and 100 video teachings, many of which have been translated and published in more than 100 languages. His daily radio broadcast is translated into Arabic, Chinese (Amoy, Cantonese, Mandarin, Shanghaiese, Swatow), Croatian, German, Malagasy, Mongolian, Russian, Samoan, Spanish and Tongan. The radio program continues to touch lives around the world.

Derek Prince Ministries persists in reaching out to believers in over 140 countries with Derek's teachings, fulfilling the mandate to keep on "until Jesus returns." This is effected through the outreaches of more than 30 Derek Prince offices around the world, including primary work in Australia, Canada, China, France, Germany, the Netherlands, New Zealand, Norway, Russia, South Africa, Switzerland, the United Kingdom and the United States. For current information about these and other worldwide locations, visit www.derekprince.com.

Get the Complete Laying the Foundations Series

1. Founded on the Rock (B100)
2. Authority and Power of God's Word (B101)
3. Through Repentance to Faith (B102)
4. Faith and Works (B103)
5. The Doctrine of Baptisms (B104)
6. Immersion in The Spirit (B105)
7. Transmitting God's Power (B106)
8. At the End of Time (B107)
9. Resurrection of the Body (B108)
10. Final Judgment (B109)

DEREK PRINCE MINISTRIES-UK

KINGSFIELD, HADRIAN WAY

BALDOCK, SG7 6AN

HERTS, UK

WWW.DPMUK.ORG

DEREK PRINCE MINISTRIES
OFFICES WORLDWIDE

ASIA/ PACIFIC
DPM–Asia/Pacific
38 Hawdon Street, Sydenham
Christchurch 8023,
New Zealand
T: + 64 3 366 4443
E: admin@dpm.co.nz
W: www.dpm.co.nz and
www.derekprince.in

AUSTRALIA
DPM–Australia
1st Floor, 134 Pendle Way
Pendle Hill
New South Wales 2145, Australia
T: + 612 9688 4488
E: enquiries@derekprince.com.au
W: www.derekprince.com.au

CANADA
DPM–Canada
P. O. Box 8354 Halifax,
Nova Scotia B3K 5M1, Canada
T: + 1 902 443 9577
E: enquiries.dpm@eastlink.ca
W: www.derekprince.org

FRANCE
DPM–France
B.P. 31, Route d'Oupia,
34210 Olonzac,
France
T: + 33 468 913872
E: info@derekprince.fr
W: www.derekprince.fr

GERMANY
DPM–Germany
Schwarzauer Str. 56
D-83308 Trostberg,
Germany
T: + 49 8621 64146
E: IBL.de@t-online.de
W: www.ibl-dpm.net

NETHERLANDS
DPM–Netherlands
P. O. Box 349
1960 AH Heemskerk,
The Netherlands
T: + 31 251 255 044
E: info@nl.derekprince.com
W: www.dpmnederland.nl

NORWAY
P. O. Box 129 Lodderfjord
N-5881, Bergen,
Norway
T: +47 928 39855
E: sverre@derekprince.no
W: www.derekprince.no

SINGAPORE
Derek Prince
Publications Pte. Ltd.
P. O. Box 2046 ,
Robinson Road Post Office
Singapore 904046
T: + 65 6392 1812
E: dpmchina@singnet.com.sg
English web: www.dpmchina.org
Chinese web: www.ygmweb.org

SOUTH AFRICA
DPM–South Africa
P. O. Box 33367
Glenstantia 0010 Pretoria
South Africa
T: +27 12 348 9537
E: enquiries@derekprince.co.za
W: www.derekprince.co.za

SWITZERLAND
DPM–Switzerland
Alpenblick 8
CH-8934 Knonau
Switzerland
T: + 41(0) 44 768 25 06
E: dpm-ch@ibl-dpm.net
W: www.ibl-dpm.net

UNITED KINGDOM
DPM–UK
Kingsfield, Hadrian Way
Baldock SG7 6AN
UK
T: + 44 (0) 1462 492100
E: enquiries@dpmuk.org
W: www.dpmuk.org

USA
DPM–USA
P. O. Box 19501
Charlotte NC 28219,
USA
T: + 1 704 357 3556
E: ContactUs@derekprince.org
W: www.derekprince.org